miffy x rem

mercis x rijksmuseum

Rembrandt and Dick Bruna are both Dutch and both world famous. In this book you will find lots of the wonderful works they created.

Although their pictures may look very different, lots of things are the same. They both painted people, animals and landscapes, but each did so in their own way. Join Miffy as she takes a look at Rembrandt's art and discovers similarities and differences.

Marten and Oopjen are dressed as smartly as the king and queen. Can you see what looks the same? Have you checked their shoes?

Ooh! What gave them such a fright?

We are both wearing party dresses.
Which is prettiest?

A self-portrait is a picture of yourself.
Have you ever drawn a self-portrait?

How can you stand out in a group? Do you first notice someone wearing something different? Or someone acting differently?

ÆT: 76

What is the same?
Look at the colours that have been used.

What is the old man feeling?
And what about Miffy? How are you feeling today?

Can you see the sun shining from behind the clouds?

The old lady and Miffy are both reading a book.
What is your favourite book?

Who has the nicest hat?

Do you see that big boat?
Boris would love to give it a try.

This is a painting of Miffy's friend Melanie.
The other painting is of Saskia, Rembrandt's wife.

**Dick Bruna and Rembrandt were both
very good at drawing themselves.
But why are their eyes so hard to see?**

This instrument is called a cello.
It makes beautiful music.
Do you see the cello in the painting?

This is Rembrandt's son Titus.
He isn't looking at us, just like Miffy.

How odd! These two lions don't look very dangerous at all. Why is that?

How do you know they love each other?
Who would you like to give a big hug?

Illustrations

Rembrandt, 'Marten Soolmans and Oopjen Coppit', 1634
Joint acquisition by the Dutch State and the French Republic,
collection Rijksmuseum/collection Musée du Louvre
Dick Bruna, The prince dancing with Cinderella, from
'Cinderella', 1966

Rembrandt, 'Self-Portrait with Beret, Wide-Eyed', 1630
Dick Bruna, Aggie and Winnie are frightened, from
'Miffy the ghost', 2001

Rembrandt, 'Portrait of a Woman, probably Maria Trip', 1639
On loan from the Familie Van Weede Stichting
Dick Bruna, Miffy in her party dress, from 'Miffy's birthday',
1970

Rembrandt, 'Self-Portrait of Rembrandt, Etching at
a Window', 1648
Mr and Mrs De Bruijn-van der Leeuw Bequest, Muri,
Switzerland
Dick Bruna, Draw, from 'When I grow up', 1980

Rembrandt, 'The Sampling Officials of the Amsterdam
Drapers' Guild', known as 'The Syndics', 1662
On loan from the City of Amsterdam
Dick Bruna, Reading to the class, from 'Miffy at school', 1984

Rembrandt, 'Portrait of Johannes Wtenbogaert', 1633
Purchased with the support of the Rembrandt Association,
with additional funding from the Prins Bernhard Cultuurfonds,
the VSBfonds, the Stichting tot Bevordering van de Belangen
van het Rijksmuseum, the State of the Netherlands and
private collectors
Dick Bruna, Judge, from 'What we're going to be', 1996

Rembrandt, 'Jeremiah Lamenting the Destruction
of Jerusalem', 1630
Purchased with the support of private collectors,
the Rembrandt Association and the Stichting tot
Bevordering van de Belangen van het Rijksmuseum
Dick Bruna, Miffy is thinking, from 'Flopear', 2006

Rembrandt, 'Landscape with a Stone Bridge', c. 1638
Purchased with the support of the Rembrandt
Association and A. Bredius, Amsterdam
Dick Bruna, Sun behind the clouds, from
'Boris on the mountain', 1989

Rembrandt, 'Old Woman Reading', 1631
Dick Bruna, Miffy is reading, autonomous work, 1982

Rembrandt, 'Officers and Other Civic Guardsmen of
District II in Amsterdam, under the Command of Captain
Frans Banninck Cocq and Lieutenant Willem van
Ruytenburch', known as 'The Night Watch', 1642
On loan from the City of Amsterdam
Front cover: **Dick Bruna**, Miffy looking at art, from
'Miffy at the gallery', 1997
Inside: **Dick Bruna**, Miffy and friends dancing,
autonomous work, 2002

Rembrandt, 'Man in Oriental Dress', 1635
Gift of Mr and Mrs Kessler-Hülsmann, Kapelle op den Bosch
Dick Bruna, Betty's birthday, from 'The school', 1964

Rembrandt, 'Canal with a Large Boat and a Bridge', 1650
Dick Bruna, Boris in his boat, from 'Boris Bear's boat', 1996

Rembrandt, 'Bust of a Young Woman in Fantasy
Costume', 1633
Mr and Mrs De Bruijn-van der Leeuw Bequest, Muri,
Switzerland
Dick Bruna, Framed picture of Melanie, from
'Miffy and Melanie', 1999

Rembrandt, 'Self-Portrait', c. 1628
Purchased with the support of the Rembrandt Association,
the Stichting tot Bevordering van de Belangen van het
Rijksmuseum and the Ministry of Culture, Recreation and
Social Work
Dick Bruna, Self-portrait, autonomous work, 1991

Rembrandt, 'Musical Company', 1626
Purchased with the support of the Rembrandt Association
and the Stichting tot Bevordering van de Belangen van het
Rijksmuseum
Dick Bruna, Sally plays the cello, from 'The orchestra', 1984

Rembrandt, 'Rembrandt's Son Titus in a Monk's Habit', 1660
Purchased with the support of the Rembrandt Association,
1933; formerly Stroganoff Collection, St Petersburg
Dick Bruna, Miffy gets tired, from 'Miffy', 1963

Rembrandt (school of), 'Reclining Lion', c. 1650
Mr and Mrs De Bruijn-van der Leeuw Bequest, Muri,
Switzerland
Dick Bruna, L is for lion, from 'B is for bear', 1967

Rembrandt, 'Isaac and Rebecca',
known as 'The Jewish Bride', c. 1665
On loan from the City of Amsterdam
(A. van der Hoop bequest)
Dick Bruna, Miffy and her friend, from
'Miffy goes to stay', 1988

Back cover
Dick Bruna, Miffy and Mother Bunny,
from 'Miffy at the gallery', 1997

This book was published on the occasion
of the Year of Rembrandt 2019.

Text
Mercis Publishing bv

Translation
Richard de Nooy

Illustrations
Dick Bruna © copyright Mercis bv, 1953–2019

Photography
Image Department
of the Rijksmuseum

Design
Irma Boom Office

Lithography and Printing
Tienkamp, Groningen

Publishers
Mercis Publishing bv Amsterdam
Rijksmuseum Amsterdam

Mercis Publishing bv
Johannes Vermeerplein 3
1071 DV Amsterdam
The Netherlands

info@mercis.nl
miffy.com

Rijksmuseum
P.O. Box 74888
1070 DN Amsterdam
The Netherlands

publicaties@rijksmuseum.nl
rijksmuseum.nl

ISBN 978-90-5647-797-4
10 9 8 7 6 5 4 3 2 1

Printed and bound in the Netherlands